DISCOVERING THE UNITED STATES

Louisiana

BY IB LARSEN

An Imprint of Abdo Publishing
abdobooks.com

abdobooks.com

Published by Abdo Publishing, a division of ABDO, PO Box 398166, Minneapolis, Minnesota 55439. Copyright © 2025 by Abdo Consulting Group, Inc. International copyrights reserved in all countries. No part of this book may be reproduced in any form without written permission from the publisher. Kids Core™ is a trademark and logo of Abdo Publishing.

Printed in China.
052024
092024

Cover Photo: Shutterstock Images
Interior Photos: Chronicle/Alamy, 4–5; Shutterstock Images, 7 (top left), 16, 26, 28 (top right), 28 (bottom right); Dirk M. de Boer/Shutterstock Images, 7 (top right); Chuck Wagner/Shutterstock Images, 7 (bottom left); Aneta Jungerova/Shutterstock Images, 7 (bottom right); Ric Feld/AP Images, 9; iStockphoto, 11; Tim Mosenfelder/WireImage/Getty Images, 12–13; Lan Wei/Xinhua News Agency/Getty Images, 14; Erika Goldring/Getty Images Entertainment/Getty Images, 17; Cavan Images/Alamy, 18; Sean Pavone/Shutterstock Images, 20–21, 28 (bottom left); Bettmann/Getty Images, 22; Danita Delimont/Gallo Images Roots RF Collection/Getty Images, 25; GTS Productions/Shutterstock Images, 27; Red Line Editorial, 28 (top left), 29

Editor: Laura Stickney
Series Designer: Katharine Hale

Library of Congress Control Number: 2023949334

Publisher's Cataloging-in-Publication Data

Names: Larsen, Ib, author.
Title: Louisiana / by Ib Larsen
Description: Minneapolis, Minnesota: Abdo Publishing, 2025 | Series: Discovering the United States | Includes online resources and index.
Identifiers: ISBN 9781098293888 (lib. bdg.) | ISBN 9798384913153 (ebook)
Subjects: LCSH: U.S. states--Juvenile literature. | Louisiana--History--Juvenile literature. | Southeastern States--Juvenile literature. | Physical geography--United States--Juvenile literature.
Classification: DDC 973--dc23

All population data taken from:
"Estimates of Population by Sex, Race, and Hispanic Origin: April 1, 2020 to July 1, 2022." *US Census Bureau, Population Division*, June 2023, census.gov.

CONTENTS

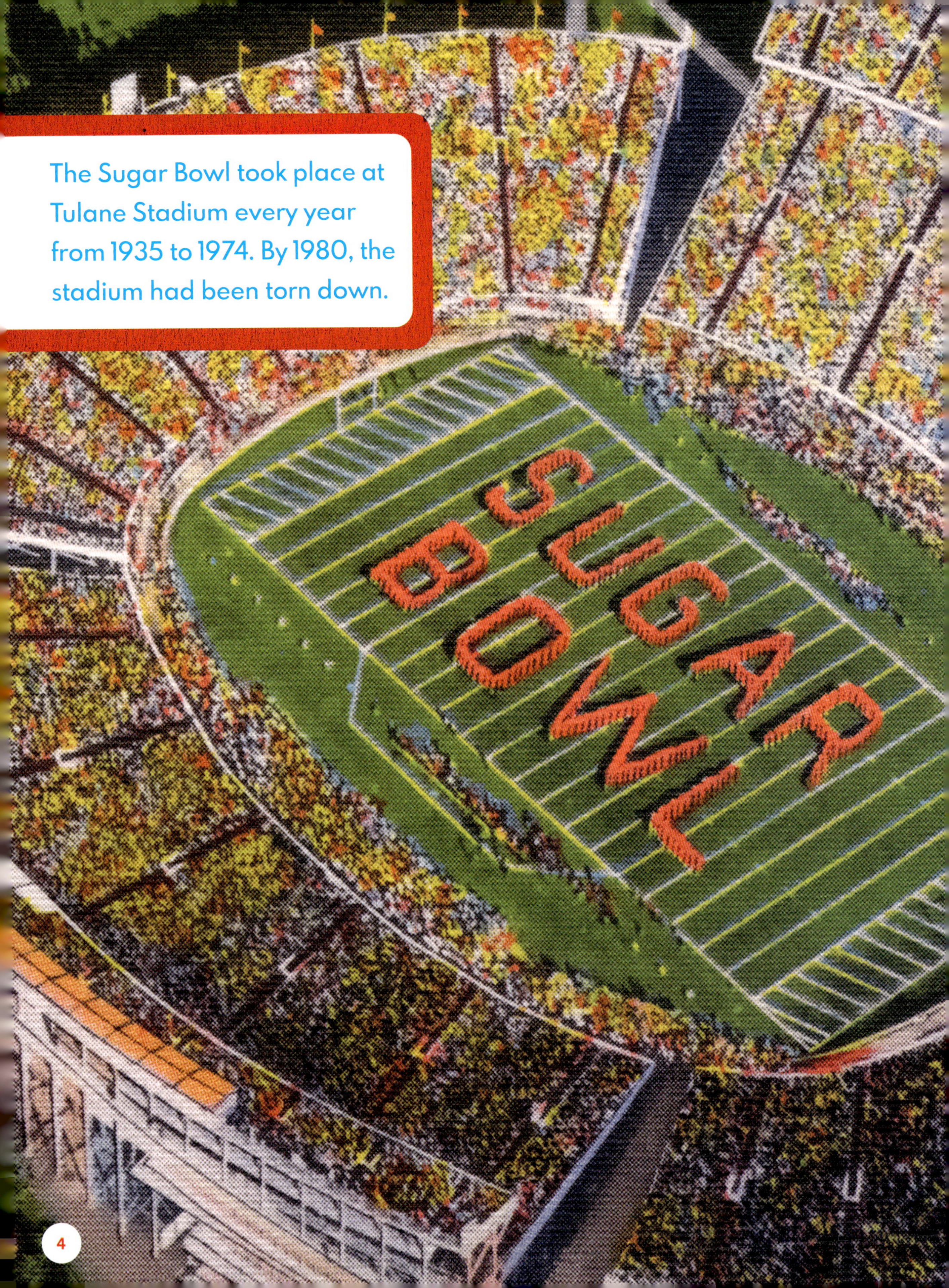

The Sugar Bowl took place at Tulane Stadium every year from 1935 to 1974. By 1980, the stadium had been torn down.

The Sugar Bowl

It was New Year's Day in 1935. The first Sugar Bowl football game was about to begin in New Orleans, Louisiana. More than 22,000 people gathered at Tulane Stadium. The home team of Tulane University would be playing Temple University.

This team was from Philadelphia, Pennsylvania. Many people expected Tulane University to lose the game. When the game started, Temple University took an early two-touchdown lead. It seemed like Tulane would lose the game.

But then something incredible happened. Tulane's Johnny McDaniel received the kickoff and tricked the defense by passing the ball to Claude Simons Jr. Some well-timed blocks allowed Simons to run the ball to Temple's end zone. Tulane was back in the game. Soon, the team was a touchdown ahead of Temple. At the end of the game, the score was 20–14. Tulane had won the Sugar Bowl.

The Sugar Bowl is held in New Orleans every year around New Year's Day. It is

Louisiana Facts

DATE OF STATEHOOD
April 30, 1812

CAPITAL
Baton Rouge

POPULATION
4,590,241

AREA
52,378 square miles (135,658 sq km)

STATE BIRD

Brown pelican

STATE TREE

Bald cypress

STATE FLOWER

Magnolia

STATE DOG

Catahoula leopard dog

Each US state has a different population, size, and capital city. States also have state symbols.

one of Louisiana's biggest sporting events. The eighty-ninth Sugar Bowl was held on December 31, 2022. More than 60,000 people attended.

Land and Wildlife

Louisiana is in the US region called the South. Mississippi lies to the east of the state. Arkansas borders it to the north. To the west is Texas. Louisiana's southern coastline borders the Gulf of Mexico.

The land near the Gulf Coast is low and swampy. Unique plants and animals live there.

Alligators

There are more than 2 million alligators in Louisiana. They live in bodies of water such as lakes and swamps. Cypress Lake is a small lake at the University of Louisiana in the city of Lafayette. People can stand on a deck and look for alligators creeping through the water.

In 2005, Hurricane Katrina hit near the city of New Orleans. More than 80 percent of the city was flooded because of the storm, and many homes were destroyed.

Spanish moss hangs off the branches of bald cypress trees. Alligators, shrimp, and **crayfish** swim in the water. The largest lake in Louisiana is Lake Pontchartrain. The Mississippi River flows into the Gulf of Mexico through Louisiana. This makes the soil in the southern part of the state very **fertile**. Farmers use this land to grow crops. In northern Louisiana, the land is hilly.

Climate

Louisiana summers are long and very **humid**. Winters are short, and snow is rare. Cold, dry air from the north meets warm, wet air from the Gulf of Mexico. This causes many thunderstorms. Hurricanes can strike Louisiana's shore anytime between June and November.

Further Evidence

Look at the website below. Does it give any new evidence to support Chapter One?

Louisiana

abdocorelibrary.com/discovering-louisiana

Bald cypress trees grow well in wet, swampy parts of Louisiana.

American Indians in Louisiana celebrate their cultural traditions at the annual New Orleans Jazz and Heritage Festival. In 2023, the event featured traditional music and dancing.

The People of Louisiana

People have lived in Louisiana since around 11,500 BCE. Many American Indian nations have called the state home. These include the Chitimacha, Atakapa, Caddo, Choctaw, and Natchez peoples. They hunted and farmed crops.

Today, many people in Louisiana celebrate Juneteenth. On June 19, 1865, the Emancipation Proclamation was enforced in Texas. Many enslaved people learned they had been freed.

Louisiana is known for its **diverse** population. In the 1700s and 1800s, settlers from France, Spain, and Britain came to the state.

White Europeans enslaved African people and brought them to Louisiana to work on farms.

In 2022, 58 percent of people in Louisiana were white. About 33 percent were Black. Six percent of the population was Hispanic or Latino, and about 2 percent was Asian. American Indians made up about 1 percent of the population.

The Louisiana Purchase

Thomas Jefferson was US president from 1801 to 1809. One of his goals was for the United States to purchase the Louisiana **Territory** from France This took place in 1803. The territory included what is now Louisiana. The purchase of this land is called the Louisiana Purchase. The land was later separated into parts of 15 states.

Louisiana's state flag features a white pelican and three pelican chicks in a nest.

Culture

Many people in Louisiana identify with Creole culture. This includes elements of French, African, and American Indian cultures. Jambalaya is a Creole food that is popular in Louisiana. It is made by cooking meat, vegetables, and rice in a pot. The po' boy sandwich is another common Creole food. It consists of meat served with toppings on fluffy French bread.

Groups of people called krewes hold big parades during Mardi Gras. Krewe members toss beads, toys, and treats to people in the crowd.

Another part of Louisiana's culture is Mardi Gras. This holiday is celebrated every year, 47 days before Easter. Many cities have Mardi Gras parades. People wear costumes and follow parade **floats** through the city's streets.

Some workers in Louisiana drill for oil and natural gas in the Gulf of Mexico. Offshore drilling requires setting up large rigs in the water.

Industry

Many people in Louisiana have jobs drilling for oil and natural gas. Other people **manufacture** chemicals. Some people cut down trees for wood. In New Orleans, many people provide services for the city's large number of visitors. They work in hotels and restaurants.

New Orleans resident Sarah Barnett celebrates Mardi Gras. She said:

> I grew up going to parades with my family. There's just something special about Mardi Gras when you head back to the same spots each year to watch the parades.

Source: Forrest Brown. "Mardi Gras 2023: Big Easy Returns to Playing Hard. Here's What You Need to Know." *CNN*, 20 Feb. 2023, cnn.com. Accessed 21 Sept. 2023.

What's the Big Idea?

What is this quote's main idea? Explain how the main idea is supported by details.

In New Orleans, visitors can ride historic streetcars along Canal Street. This street has many shops, hotels, and theaters.

CHAPTER 3

Places in Louisiana

Louisiana's capital is Baton Rouge. But New Orleans is the state's largest city. Other major cities include Shreveport and Lafayette. Many of Louisiana's cities were founded by French settlers. New Orleans is named after the French Duke of Orléans.

Louis Armstrong Park honors the famous jazz musician who was born in New Orleans.

Parks

The New Orleans Jazz National Historical Park is in the center of the city. It celebrates the musical **genre** of jazz. The park is located in the city's Louis Armstrong Park. Park officials host jazz concerts there. Visitors can learn about jazz at the nearby visitor center.

Louisiana has many state parks too. Fontainebleau State Park is on the coast of Lake Pontchartrain. A trail passes through the park.

Louis Armstrong

Many great jazz musicians were born in New Orleans. Louis Armstrong is one of the most famous. He played the trumpet and sang. He is known for songs such as "What a Wonderful World" and "West End Blues."

Signs on the trail teach visitors about the different birds and animals that live in the area. At Chicot State Park, visitors can ride mountain bikes on hilly trails. The park also includes swamps. Some people fish in the swampy waters.

Landmarks

One of the most visited landmarks in Louisiana is the French Quarter. This is the oldest neighborhood in downtown New Orleans. It was built by French settlers. People visit the French Quarter to see its colorful buildings.

Another landmark is the Poverty Point World Heritage Site. American Indians built mounds of earth at the site about 3,400 years ago. No one

Visitors of Louisiana state parks might spot alligators in the swampy waters. Fontainebleau State Park has an Alligator Marsh Boardwalk for wildlife viewing.

knows exactly what the mounds were for. Some believe people lived and traded on them. Visitors can take guided tours to learn more about the mounds.

The USS *Kidd* is named after Isaac C. Kidd, a US soldier who was killed during World War II. Near the ship is a memorial for Louisiana service members.

In Baton Rouge, people can visit the USS *Kidd*. This is a large ship that was used in World War II (1939–1945). Visitors can tour the ship and explore a nearby museum.

Louisiana is a state with a lot of charm. Its natural beauty and unique culture attracts many visitors. People can spend time outdoors

The French Quarter is known for its historic French and Spanish buildings. The neighborhood is home to many shops, cafes, and restaurants.

in Louisiana's state parks. Or they can visit the state's most interesting cities and towns. There's something for everyone in Louisiana.

Explore Online

Visit the website below. Does it give any new information about New Orleans that wasn't in Chapter Three?

New Orleans

abdocorelibrary.com/discovering-louisiana

State Map

KEY

Capital | Park

City or town | Point of interest

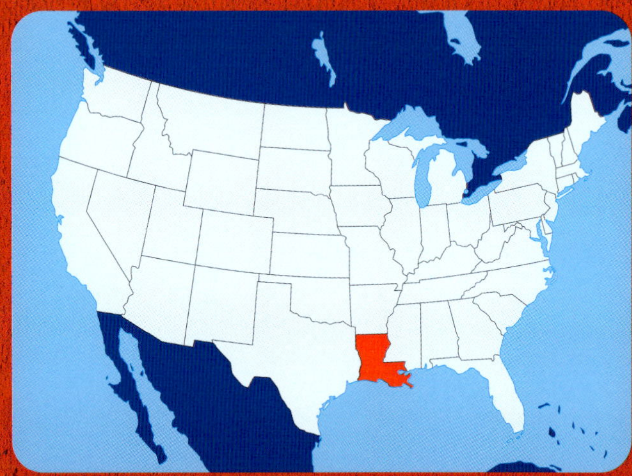

USS *Kidd*

Chicot State Park

New Orleans

Louisiana: The Pelican State
Arkansas
Shreveport
Lake Claiborne
Lake Claiborne State Park
Poverty Point World Heritage Site
N
W
E
S
Mississippi
Mississippi River
Texas
Baton Rouge
Fontainebleau State Park
Chicot State Park
USS Kidd
Lake Pontchartrain
Lafayette
New Orleans
French Quarter
New Orleans Jazz National Historical Park
Fort Jackson
Gulf of Mexico

Glossary

crayfish
lobsterlike animals that live in fresh water

diverse
having many different kinds of people

fertile
able to produce healthy plant growth

floats
decorated stages pulled through parades

genre
a grouping of artwork made in a similar style

humid
describing air that has a lot of moisture

manufacture
to make goods to sell

territory
a particular area of land that belongs to and is governed by a country

Online Resources

To learn more about Louisiana, visit our free resource websites below.

Visit **abdocorelibrary.com** or scan this QR code for free Common Core resources for teachers and students, including vetted activities, multimedia, and booklinks, for deeper subject comprehension.

Visit **abdobooklinks.com** or scan this QR code for free additional online weblinks for further learning. These links are routinely monitored and updated to provide the most current information available.

Learn More

Abdo, Kenny. *Jazz Music History*. Abdo, 2020.

Murray, Julie. *Louisiana*. Abdo, 2020.

Weston, Margeaux, and Sarosh Arif. *We Are the United States*. Wide Eyed Editions, 2022.

Index

About the Author

Ib Larsen is a writer and editorial assistant living in Saint Paul, Minnesota.